Withdrawn From Stock
Dublin City Libraries

Withdrawn From Stock
Dublin City Libraries

All Will Be Well

First published in 2017
by columba press
23 Merrion Square
Dublin 2, Ireland
www.columba.ie

Copyright © 2017 Paddy Byrne

All rights reserved. Without limiting the rights under copyright reserved alone, no part of this publication may be reproduced, stored in or introduced into a retrieval system, or transmitted, in any form or by any means (electronic, mechanical, photocopying, recording or otherwise) without the prior written permission of both the copyright owner and the above publisher of the book.

ISBN: 978 1 78218 303 7

Set in Linux Libertine 12/16
Cover and book design by Alba Esteban | Columba Press
Printed by ScandBook, Sweden

All Will Be Well

Paddy Byrne

Leabharlanna Poibli Chathair Baile Átha Cliath
Dublin City Public Libraries

To my Mum and Dad

Contents

Part 4:
Reflections and inspirations

Part 5:
Parables and prayers

Introduction

Social media is part of all our lives. As a minister of the Gospel, I welcome every opportunity to engage with people. My social network of choice is Twitter. My Twitter account is @frpaddybyrne. My followers are like an online parish to which I tweet positive messages about life and comments about issues of social justice. I have experienced extraordinary moments of connection and deep spiritual conversion thanks to my Twitter account. I have even celebrated the marriage of several Twitter connections. I am amazed and delighted with the number of followers the account has attracted.

For the past ten years, I have been a columnist for *The Laois and Carlow Nationalist.* I also post a weekly blog to our local parish publication, *The Link Up,* and the Portlaoise Parish website (www.portlaoiseparish.ie). The Church has failed so often in its duty to communicate to the masses. The Church here often speaks on the defensive and is much too hesitant to engage in conversation on local or national radio about real issues such as homelessness and human vulnerability. It has been a very positive experience for me to contribute to both national and local media outlets. After all, as a Christian follower, I'm called to get out there and share the Good News.

The reason I tweet, the reason I blog and the reason I wrote this book are the same: I hope that I can somehow help people in their daily journeys. Life, as we all know, brings many challenges, and sometimes a reminder to 'take a deep breath this too will pass' can be a great help to someone who may be overwhelmed. Speaking in Knock in 1979, Pope Saint John Paul II said, 'Every generation is like a new continent to be won for Christ'. The digital world, which is so much a part of life for younger generations, presents the kind of challenge Pope Saint John Paul II referred to. I hope through this modest volume to share the Good News and to point to the Good in life.

Count your Blessings

I hope that this book might encourage you to count your blessings. Sometimes life can seem challenging, and we often experience the well-known feeling that the grass is always greener elsewhere or in someone else's life. If we think very deeply, we will realise that our life is full of blessings. We are so immersed in our busy life that we hardly recognise them.

When this happens, the best thing to do is to close

your eyes and start counting all the blessings that God has given you. When you go out for a drive, roll down the window and look at the poor beggar standing under the hot sun, begging so that he might fill his hungry stomach. We get three meals a day; isn't that a blessing?

Whenever you are sad, look in the eyes of family members. Their eyes are filled with love and concern for you. There are many people who have never experienced the love of a family. Isn't that a blessing? Our lives are full of such blessings in disguise; all we have to do is to discover them.

Life is all about helping others. When we love people without any expectations and we help them, our heart is filled with an immense sense of happiness. Seeing the contented smile on someone's face and the gratefulness in their eyes can bring great peace. Mother Teresa said, 'We don't need to do great things. We need to do small things with great love'.

Think of life like this:

L - Live

I - It to the

F - Fullest

E - Extent

And the next time life knocks you down, close your eyes and start counting!

Part 1
My life journey

1

The sacred gift of family

Family is a sacred gift. Family provides a place where we hopefully enjoy a sense of belonging, a connection that bonds us closely together. Family is home, though of course family brings with it its challenges. I'm very proud to belong to a family where I feel loved and treasured. In my adult life, I recognise the huge sacrifices that were made to provide for my siblings and me.

I am a twin and as a twin I never fully identified as a single unit, life for me has always been in the company of another. As an adult, I often find within myself the strong need for company. I am a natural extrovert and find strength in relating to others. My brother Noel is my 'anam cara' *(Soul mate in Irish).* Our birth was a great surprise; our mother hadn't a clue that she was carrying twins. Labour came very early and she was rushed to Kilkenny hospital by a neighbour, Michael Townsend, one of the few people in our estate who had a car. On 17

March 1974, babies Noel and Patrick were born, 2.5lbs and 3lbs respectively. At home, my father Noel celebrated St Patrick's Day with my siblings Ken, Jimmy and Esther. My sister Esther cried for two days; she was so disappointed that she had no baby sister.

My mother Margaret (or Peg to her family) was a remarkable woman. I remember jumping into my parents' bed with my twin brother and playing a nursery rhyme about little piggies with our toes. Saturday night was bath night, and to check that we passed the test for cleanliness, we would have to open our toes. If any dirt appeared, it was back up to the bath again. I remember sitting beside the fire on those Saturday nights in what now seems like a very small sitting room. Back then though, it was such an all-encompassing place surrounded by the warmth and love of my parents. My mother in particular had a very strong faith. Our days would end in prayer. It just happened. It seemed normal. We often interrupted and protested as we grew older but the rhythm of our household facilitated prayer. Both my parents publicly practiced their faith. I have a distinct memory as a child listening to my mother saying her night prayers too, at length and out loud from her bedroom.

My father Noel was a rather childlike character, colourful, humorous and certainly full of surprises. He was also a man who carried the cross of alcoholism throughout his life. This vulnerability of his made me keenly aware from a young age that he needed extra support and minding. As is common in situations of addiction, the child parents the adult. This role catapulted me to a place of maturity and sensitivity well beyond my childhood years. It also gave me a sensitivity that remains with me in ministry and helps me to support and encourage those I encounter who are living with the reality of addiction. As I grew into adulthood, my dad became a friend, never someone who let me down because of his addiction. My father had a wonderful, creative imagination. He loved swimming, and I cherish a particular memory from our annual visit to Courtown when I was five. We would go out into the sea, me holding on to his back and his shoulders for dear life and trusting him because, he told us, he once swam from 'Wexford to England'. He would tell us about the killer sharks beneath us! Many Carlowvians will remember learning how to swim in the river Burren. To prevent us from messing, when our father brought us there, he would remind us of a certain Sally hole, that is, an unknown spot in the river filled with quick sand. If we went in too deep, we would never return.

My grandmother (whom we lovingly called Ma Lennon) was a great presence in my life. She died at the ripe old age of 99. She was one of the wisest and resilient women I have ever known. Together with my granddad, she farmed land in a place called Knockbawn, Old Leighlin, Co. Carlow. In a small thatch household indicative of the time, she reared a large family, living to see seventy-nine grandchildren. She had a tough life. Her work ethic and deep resilient spirit transcended the many challenges that were put before her. She had a wonderful sense of humour and a wisdom that was remarkable. I remember her visits to our family home on Mondays, the days of the local mart and cattle sales. She took a keen interest during haymaking and harvest time. She never wasted anything and in her later years, appreciated the basic luxuries (such as electricity, telephones, running water) that for most of her life were a distant reality.

My fathers parents both died when I was young but my aunts and uncles were very much part of my life. My father's brother Billy was fond of hunting and occasionally we would be brought with him. Billy's wife Marie was a great cook and my dad often brought us up for a random visit at lunchtime. My uncle Michael and my aunt Mary were like second parents to us. Both of them had no children and they were very kind to our needs. My aunt Eithne always called to our home. She introduced us children to coffee, which we never were allowed to have. My uncle Oliver, my godfather, and my aunt Judy were a wonderful example of marriage, particularly in their later years. Oliver was a true gentleman. He was selfless and his great affection for Judy made her feel safe and at home, even when she developed Alzheimer's. I'm proud to be his godson.

I grew up in a very working-class housing estate in Carlow town. It was a wonderful place where neighbours knew and cared for each other. At the same time, it was a place crippled by unemployment, lack of educational opportunities and addiction. Then, as now, the well-off have greater pathways of opportunity, whereas those who are not are at greater risk of dropping out of mainstream education or entering into pathways of addiction. It was and is the vicious circle that we now call cyclical disadvantage. I have yet to see a radical investment aiming to break that cycle. Last year shamefully highlighted the devastation of homelessness and growing poverty. The government's 'Keep the Recovery Going' campaign for the 2016 general election is evidence of a great disconnect. Many people in places such as my Carlow estate never felt the recovery. Any minister of finance trying to balance a budget could learn from my mother. In times of huge challenge, she instilled within all of us a firm and resolute belief that hard work was the key to being liberated from disadvantage.

2
Vocation

An older priest once told me, 'The reason you stay in ministry is much different than the reason you were attracted to it in the first place'. I felt a close relationship to God from an early age. My family and church coalesced. My brothers and I were altar servers in Carlow Cathedral. Our family enjoyed a positive relationship with the priests of our parish. I remember being particularly inspired by the late Fr John Fingleton, a priest who gave a wonderful service to the people of Carlow. His presence was warm and friendly. He was a deeply spiritual man. I remember being brought with my twin brother Noel to the Poor Clare Convent in Graiguecullen, Carlow, on my first Holy Communion day, to see an enclosed order of sisters whose spirituality was contemplative and so inspirational. Looking at them through a grail was something very mysterious. The place was silent and yet full of the strong presence of Christ. I also remember receiving holy medals and, more importantly, a Milky Bar in honour of my first Communion. It was great joy for me to be able to celebrate Mass with the good sisters shortly after my ordination to the priesthood.

I remember in my teenage years feeling awkward about my relationship with the Church and about being a member of the folk group in the cathedral. Even then, it wasn't cool for young people to be part of the Church. Deep down I had the sense that the life of a priest was deeply necessary and relevant, not just for the celebration of the sacraments, but as a presence to any faith community. The priest is a presence that offers support, encouragement, consolation and solidarity at key moments in people's lives. Huge scandals were already beginning to emerge and in truth I was afraid to name a deep desire within me. I heard Christ calling me to live a life of service as a priest. I knew my parents would react positively, but fear and a sense of confusion made me silent.

After my Leaving Cert, an exam to which I applied myself wholeheartedly, I went to Trinity College to study business, economics and social studies. Trinity was a wonderful place, though it was not easy for me to integrate. It was certainly during this time that the desire to do something with my life intensified and drove me to make contact with the local vocations director, Fr John Dunphy. Fr Dunphy listened to me and helped me make sense of the way I felt.

In September 1994 I finally entered the seminary in Carlow College, which was three minutes from my home in Hanover and yet felt like another planet. My mother sensed that this new journey would be a difficult one and in her wisdom she assured me of her constant prayer and support. My father, a more silent man, placed this letter under my pillow the night before I entered the seminary.

16 September 1994

Patrick,
I hope that you will always be happy, and if your choice in life is for God then always do the very best you can. Patrick, you will always come up with doubts and wonder if your decision is the right one. Always pray and God will direct you in the right way. Do not worry about Mammy or the family; everything will turn out right, please God. All I can say is that I am proud of you and that you followed your intention. I urge you; when you have many doubts and are under any pressure, pray hard for guidance and God will reveal the right pathway to you. All you can do is your best and this is all any of us is asked for. You will always have a home here in Hanover. I love you and as you know your Mammy, Jimmy, Esther, Kenneth and Noel love you also. Pray hard.

Daddy

I often read this letter; it personifies what many spiritual writers call 'the wounded healer'. Our best insights in life often come from wounded people. Perhaps that's why the risen Christ presented his wounds to Thomas so that Thomas might believe. My wounded father shared this testimony of faith and insight with me, so that I too may believe that our God is the giver of all gifts, the source of our hope and indeed the true pathway.

Carlow College in 1994 was embracing a new model for the Church. Monsignor Kevin O'Neill was leading this change. Monsignor O'Neill was a prophetic voice, who saw the necessity for preparing men for priesthood in a Church that would be smaller in terms of clerical numbers but stronger in pastoral presence, a Church comfortable to engage not in black-and-white certainties, but in the greyness of uncertainty and change; a Church trying to build bridges in the diversity of a modern Ireland rather than trying to build a wall of defence. Carlow College broadened my vision and encouraged a bold and radical witness of authentic faith, in a spirit like that of the early Church. My time in the seminary also allowed me to grow in my faith with so many wonderful fellow pilgrims, lay young men and women engaging with the same philosophical and theological questions.

My formator for many years, Fr Con Ó Maoldmhnaigh, again offered tremendous encouragement and support in discerning my vocation to the priesthood. He was patient with me during my own search, validated my authenticity and at all times challenged the reality of life in its many complexities. In 1994, nine of us began this discernment pathway; four of us are now serving in the priesthood. I learned to grow in personal confidence during my formation. There was a wonderful team to support and encourage us on our journey. The seminary was not a place to disengage from the reality of life. It was far from the monastic model that failed in so many ways to equip priests for the reality of life outside the walls. At all times in our formation, we engaged in many pastoral projects: teaching in schools, working in parishes, visiting prisons, working as chaplains in hospitals. For me, it became clear that I loved this way of life; I loved the energy, dynamism and diversity in parish life. In prayer and reflection, I enjoyed an inner peace, hopefulness and certainty that this was indeed the right pathway for me. Yes, I was very young, naïve, and perhaps too certain. But I was fuelled with a genuine energy from the Lord to embrace the priesthood. During that time, a thirty-day silent retreat in Manresa, the Jesuit prayer centre in Dublin, brought with it a renewed clarity and acceptance about the fact that this pathway was for me.

I spent my fourth year of formation on a pastoral placement in Baltinglass Co. Wicklow, working with Fr Larry Malone and the late Fr Gary Doyle. It was a wonderful time in my life. I took to it like a duck to water. I was guided pastorally by both priests and felt deeply contented in a pastoral setting. Some memories stay with me forever. I remember Fr Gary, an elderly parish priest who loved to smoke Sweet Aftons at breakfast and coughed like his lungs were truly choked. Despite a rather stern exterior, he was a deeply compassionate man, a visionary who established a centre for people who live with the challenges of special needs. He taught me about sheep and lambs. He had invented lagging jackets for newly born lambs as a source of income to support a special needs centre. He kindly taught me how to drive, and patiently withheld criticism of my fairly pathetic efforts.

I remember Christmas Eve 1998. A brutal storm cut out all electricity in Baltinglass. I found myself somewhat alone, cold and definitely without much Christmas spirit. I knocked on the door of Fr Gary's sitting room to see him sitting by a fire, smoking. I asked if I could sit with him and remarked how lonely this Christmas Eve was. His response has stayed with me. 'You better get used to it'. Miraculously, a loud knock on the door ten minutes later, to my great joy, revealed my father Paddy. He said, 'Your Mammy's in the car. You're coming home for Christmas with us'. It was the best Christmas present I ever received. Without my family and their wonderful support, I would have been lost during my time in the seminary. I owe a huge debt of gratitude to my twin brother Noel. He was working in Superquinn Carlow during my formation, and was so very kind to me. The endless amount of fivers and tenners he gave me will never be repaid. (He had always been physically stronger and a lot tougher than me, so even as a teenager, I relied on him; there was no fear of being bullied in school or on the street because my twin would defend me 100 per cent.)

After ordination to the Diaconate in 2000, I spent four months in Cork for a clinical pastoral education course in the university hospital. It was a very challenging place but yet again, as at other moments throughout my priesthood, I found inspiration and consolation in accompanying the sick and terminally ill. As part of this programme, I served as chaplain to people who lived with cancer. I will always remember and cherish the memory of a man named Tommy. Tommy was born during a time when not having a father brought terrible stigma. He was born in a Magdalene laundry. He spoke little of his past. I do know he lived on a farm in West Cork, where he essentially worked as a child servant. All he remembered was hard work. He never experienced family or friendship in the way most of us take for granted. At sixteen, he went to London, and for forty years, he worked and drank excessively, no doubt lonely. He returned to Cork living in very poor conditions. He had pancreatic cancer. My pastoral connection to him was our mutual interest in horses. I think that 'the God question' never really came up between us but that God was powerfully present in the empathy and affection between a young gospel minister and a dying man with no other visitors. I had the privilege of holding Tommy's hand when he left this life. Tommy's parting instilled me with a realisation that God is powerfully present to the terminally ill, and that though life seems cruel and unkind to many people, it is a powerful gift. To hold Tommy's hand was the greatest gift of my formation to the priesthood. I learned, as Christ teaches by his example in the Gospel, that in giving we receive and in embracing the wounds of another we are healed.

3
Priesthood

So many people perceive the priesthood to be in crisis, certainly since the time I began my formation twenty-two years ago. I have become accustomed to a Church marred by scandal and ridicule – regrettably so, and often of its own doing. It is an institution that, though ailing, is still not prepared to let go and embrace a new model. The Church is not dead, but the model we operate with needs to die. The Church holds the wonderful, positive and healing light of Jesus Christ. Christ's light is brighter than any dysfunction or error committed by an institution that failed to put its members before its orders, and that somehow became blinded by its power.

I was ordained to the priesthood on 24 June 2001 on a sunny Sunday evening in Carlow Cathedral. The morning of my ordination, I went for a long walk with my father down the old railway line, close to where as children he brought us to swim by the River Burren. I can't remember the conversation, but I remember that the experience of that morning was most pleasant, and that it calmed my nerves before I headed down to the cathedral. My parents' housing estate, Hanover, was covered in flags and bunting. Later that week I would celebrate Mass on the green for all the community of Hanover. I was ordained by Bishop Larry Ryan. I will always treasure his gentle leadership and encouragement to me in my formation. The cathedral was packed. I remember lying prostrate on a cold floor, somewhat numbed by the occasion and trying to be present to the mystery of God's blessing unfolding. My mother and father proudly presented me with a chalice and paten. I discovered later that my mother would be paying Bramley's jewellery shop in Carlow for that chalice every week for years. Those gifts are the bread and butter of my priestly life. The Eucharist is that generous banquet through which God nourishes his people, sustaining us with hope and energy. There were wonderful celebrations in our local parish hall.

My first appointment was to Newbridge in Co. Kildare, a growing and thriving town enjoying the buzz of the Celtic Tiger. It was full of new houses erupting out of old farmlands and had effectively become a suburb of Dublin. Newbridge for me was a place of learning under the guidance of our team leader Fr Joe Mc Dermott. I couldn't have had a better mentor or friend for my first five years of priesthood. Joe was generous with his time, helping me to learn from my mistakes. Newbridge was a place where I forged many friendships and immersed myself in every aspect of ministry. It was a positive experience of working as a team, witnessing the importance of communication and reflecting on our ministerial responsibilities. One's twenties and thirties are full of enthusiasm and innocence. Our parishes regrettably do not have this experience anymore. I remember a lady in Newbridge, who on one of my first few days complained that the bishop sent the parish priests who were too young and clueless. I'm sure that now, in 2017, my local bishop, Denis Nulty, would love to have such a challenge.

The greatest gift for me in my five years spent in Newbridge was the friendship in our home in Chapel Lane. I was fortunate to share the house with Fr Liam Morgan. The matriarch of the house was Queenie. She was the priests' housekeeper, a woman whose loyalty, love and constant protection was really necessary. She was a marvellous cook and took great pride when I put on a stone and a half in the first nine months in the parish. We had a fry up in the morning, followed by a little nap, coffee at 11 a.m., a massive lunch at 1 p.m. and invariably a mighty supper at 5 p.m. The heart of our household was a retired parish priest Fr Stan Shine. Stan changed Chapel Lane from a house to a real home. He always had the fire lit. In his retirement, his ministry was counselling us younger priests and listening attentively to our issues. He was blind and grounded us in many ways as we became conscious of his needs as opposed to just our own. We concluded every day by calling into Stan's bedroom, checking that he was okay, and saying night prayer with him. I'm sure he often had it said before I would arrive home, but would be patient enough to say his prayers with me again.

Fr Stan often shared with me the story of his priestly journey. Like all of ours, it was at times very difficult. After period of deep unhappiness in Carlow College, Stan decided he had enough and headed off to London. It was not really the thing to do for a young priest in the Catholic Ireland of the 1950s. His brother, also a priest in our diocese, was given a letter by Bishop Thomas Keogh. Eventually, Stan's brother found him in London and gave him the letter. Stan opened it and read 'Come back Stan'. Fr Stan never told that story to me without deep emotion. It's a fitting story in this year of mercy. While Bishop Keogh had a reputation as an austere and strict man, for Stan he personified the loving father who went out to his prodigal son, didn't ask what he had been up to, and welcomed him home.

Change and movement is at the heart of discipleship. My second experience of parish life was in Bagnelstown, Co. Carlow. Here again, I was very happy to serve. Bagnelstown is such a beautiful parish, close to the river Barrow and Mount Leinster, and full of outstanding people, remarkable for their hospitality, kindness and encouragement. The people were so co-operative. There was an active, positive spirit in vibrant school communities and in the traditional rural areas of the parish. In a smaller place like Bagnelstown, I found it easier to get to know people at a personal level. I enjoyed many initiatives, helping out in our school musicals, saying a dawn Mass on Easter Sunday on Mount Leinster and, more than anything else, being an active presence in a part of God's vineyard that was truly so rich in bounty.

Eamonn Mahon, my neighbour across the road, and his family will always be close to my heart. Eamonn was the first to call to my door in Bagnelstown. I will never forget his opening words: 'Don't be ever on your own, Father, you have a home across the road'. Unfortunately, three years later, Eamonn died from cancer after a heroic battle. It was a privilege to have the support and friendship of Eamonn and his wife Mary.

My last four years here in Portlaoise have been the most fulfilling and happiest in my priesthood. Portlaoise is a remarkable parish with a group of people rich in faith and encouragement. There is a wonderful diversity in ministry here, from schools, sacramental preparation, prison and hospital chaplaincy... the list goes on. A parish centre is at the heart of our community. It presents a model of parish life; it is a place where the community gathers for various needs. The vision for the parish centre comes primarily from my colleague and parish priest Monsignor John

Byrne. John is a model of Church leadership. He is a wonderful team leader and true pastor, hospitable, friendly, encouraging and deeply spiritual. His leadership is exactly what is needed in so many obvious places within the Irish Church, in which such important credentials are so blatantly lacking.

I feel freer within myself, and more at peace than I have ever felt before. I believe we are on the verge of a new springtime within our Church and I sense the green shoots of its presence here in Portlaoise parish. Pope Francis is presenting a model of Church that is inclusive, necessary, and deeply inspired by its gospel foundation. That dreadful culture of clericalism thankfully no longer holds with ordinary folk. It is from below that the emergence of a new model of Church will indeed bring true renewal to its people. I'm no longer pre-occupied by fear or anxiety in relation to what it will be like in ten or twenty years' time. My fundamental task is to engage with Christ in the present moment because that's where God meets us. God never wants us to be overwhelmed by the past or to live in fear of the future; rather it's a living dynamic and encounter that is the present moment. Here in Ireland, good men like Fr Tony Flannery and Fr Brian Darcy have suffered because their prophetic voices seem to have no place in a conversation led by a fearful Church governance that was more about a cult than a living Church. It's as if there are two Churches, one that is personal and local, and the other one that seems to be somewhat removed from our reality. Fifteen years of ordination seems to have flown by, and yet I am tremendously privileged and genuinely humbled by the richness of my experience. I pray in earnest that God, who has been so good to me, might to continue to reveal his pathway.

Part 2
Powerful men and global injustice

4

The refugee crisis

President Trump's first few months in office are proving to be very worrying. I will here refer in particular to his response to the refugee crisis.

Cities in Syria are reduced to rubble. Families find themselves in a race against time, trying to rush towards safety before a razor-wire fence blocks their escape. Stories and images of the Syrian refugee crisis have flooded the news, confronting us with the heartbreaking reality of a humanitarian disaster. Yet for all of the graphic reminders and the sympathetic hand-wringing, the international community's response to the crisis has been grossly inadequate. America's response is no exception: out of 4 million Syrian refugees, the United States has accepted fewer than 1,000 for resettlement within its borders. This is a mere drop in the bucket – far less than what capacity permits and our moral responsibility demands.

The United States is among the wealthiest nations on

earth and has the largest resettlement programme in the world. President Trump's actions are frightening. The United States is a society of immigrants whose national mythology proclaims a commitment to welcoming people in need of a new start, as the inscription on the Statue of Liberty says:

Give me your tired, your poor,
Your huddled masses yearning to breathe free,
The wretched refuse of your teeming shore.
Send these, the homeless, tempest-tost to me,
I lift my lamp beside the golden door!

The United States has contributed to the violence in Syria through military and political involvement. The Syrian people have suffered under US sanctions for decades, and when these sanctions intensified in 2011 following Assad's brutal crackdown on protestors, Syrian poverty intensified along with them. The US military also provided combat training to Syrian rebels and, once the civil war was underway, 'light arms,' cash, and 'non lethal aid' to opposition fighters. In other words, the US gave enough support to continue the bloody war of attrition with government forces, but not enough to place rebels at a decisive advantage against pro-Assad forces.

The United States is a nation that prides itself on its Christian heritage and a nation in which the vast majority of people – including elected leaders – identify as Christians. If Americans in general should be welcoming Syrian refugees with open arms, then American Christians ought to be at the forefront of these efforts. Responding with compassion to strangers in need is a core of the Christian faith. The Hebrew Scriptures are a narrative saga of a refugee people. Jesus himself became a refugee when he fled with his parents as a toddler to escape genocide under Herod. The New Testament is full of the stories of early Christians who were forced to flee from one place to another to escape violence.

The people of Israel are told to 'love the alien as yourself, for you were aliens in the land of Egypt' (Leviticus 19:34). Jesus built on this longstanding tradition by declaring in Matthew 25 that whenever we welcome strangers, attending to their hunger, thirst, sickness, and poverty, we are welcoming Jesus himself. He also makes it clear that when we fail to respond to or notice those needs, we are turning our backs to the very God we claim to follow.

In the midst of the worst refugee crisis since World War II, those followers of Christ who live in a peaceful and prosperous country have a responsibility to advocate for granting asylum to more refugees, and to walk alongside them after they arrive. Through refugee sponsorship, volunteering with private resettlement agencies and providing practical support for navigating a new environment, we can put the Gospel into action. Imagine what would happen if churches across the country were willing to house refugees, drive them to medical appointments, show them around the grocery store, tutor them in English, help them register their children in school. Churches could become the extended family network that refugees need. Imagine what would happen if we recognised Jesus in these strangers from a war-torn land and came together as to welcome him into our homes and our lives.

Fewer than 1,000 refugees out of 4 million. The US can do better than this, as can we. And we must, because the lives of some of the world's most vulnerable children, women and men depend on our willingness to welcome them into the safety of our borders and help them to build a peaceful future for themselves and their families.

May we have eyes to recognise Christ in the distressing disguise of the refugees before us, and may we have the moral courage to welcome him home.

5

The Church and homosexuality: 'Who am I to judge?'

'Who am I to judge?' With those five words, spoken last year in reply to a reporter's question about the status of gay people in the Church, Pope Francis stepped away from the disapproving tone, the explicit moralising that has pushed many away from the Church. This gesture of openness, which startled the Catholic world, would prove not to be an isolated event. In a series of interviews and speeches in the first few months after his election, the Pope unilaterally declared a kind of truce in the culture wars that have divided the Vatican and much of the world. Repeatedly, he has argued that the Church's purpose was more about proclaiming God's merciful love for all people than condemning sinners for having fallen short, especially those who struggle with gender and sexual orientation. Pope Francis' approach is less ideological than intuitive, an inclusive vision of the Church centred on an identification with the poor. From this vision, theological and organisational innovations flow. I believe that the move from rule by non-negotiable imperatives to leadership by invitation and hospitality is as fundamental to the meaning of the faith as any dogma.

Pope Francis' approach is marked by compassion and understanding. In Brazil, he said, 'If a person is gay and seeks God and has good will, who am I to judge?' He also called a young gay Catholic in Toulouse who had written about his inner turmoil in reconciling his sexuality and his faith. 'Your homosexuality, it doesn't matter', Pope Francis reassured Christophe Trutino.

The Catholic Church need not abandon tradition or doctrine in order to develop and change its attitudes towards gay people or its teachings on homosexuality. Instead, it may find it is engaging with a process that is socially timely and theologically legitimate. The great nineteenth-century theologian Blessed Cardinal John Henry Newman described the way Catholic teaching becomes more detailed and explicit over time, so that later statements of doctrine can still be considered consistent with earlier statements. Newman argued that the development of doctrine could be consistent with Scripture and tradition, and that natural and beneficial consequences could be derived from reason working on the original revealed truth, drawing out consequences that at first were not obvious.

God's love is never a 'reward' for those who 'tick' the right boxes. It's a radical love, personified in Jesus Christ, whose inclusive love reaches out even more abundantly where alienation, prejudice and fear often have excluded many people from the established Church. Pope Francis says: 'The thing the Church needs most today is the ability to heal wounds and to warm the hearts of the faithful; it needs nearness, proximity. I see the Church as a field hospital after battle. It is useless to ask a seriously injured person if he has high cholesterol and about the level of his blood sugars! You have to heal his wounds. Then we can talk about everything else. Heal the wounds, heal the wounds. And you have to start from the ground up'.

In the past, I have no doubt that anyone who felt somewhat different because of his or her sexual orientation felt deeply alienated from the Church. I don't perceive Ireland's marriage equality constitutional amendment as negative. In fact, while the Church holds a definitive theology on Christian marriage, in a civil secular context, equality must at all times be affirmed. I have no doubt that many good mothers and fathers, grannies and granddads, went out to vote 'yes' in the name of a grandson, daughter, relative, neighbour or friend. For the Church's mission to be felt by all people, its basic teaching on human love, on the dignity of human person, is more important than a stifling interpretation of sexual orientation that places people on the outside.

6

Grenfell and the Good Samaritan

The Grenfell Tower inferno is not a natural tragedy. It was predicted by those best placed to know the risks. It was made possible, perhaps even inevitable, by years of governmental neglect. The Christian observing this needs to go beyond sympathising with those bereaved and offering charity to those left behind. Grenfell Tower exposes in the UK what Hurricane Katrina revealed in the USA. That was predicted by those paying attention. As the theologian Scott Prather has compellingly argued, the politics that made the tragedy of Katrina possible is one that 'seeks to profit from others' tragedy, privatise at every turn and thereby redirect political power and socio-economic resources for the material wealth of the few.'

Those who have protested the re-housing of the victims of the blaze in some of the very expensive apartment developments in Kensington have only compounded the tragedy. The call by Jeremy Corbyn to appropriate empty houses in the area for the care of those rendered homeless incited a strong negative reaction. When it emerged that the council planned to relocate some residents as far north as Preston (227 miles from London), it was made clear that there is a strand within the British government that values property rights higher than human rights.

Of course, we would be deluded if we thought that what happened in London could not happen in Ireland. We have already seen how 'self-certified' safety standards can result in buildings unfit for habitation. Even this year, we have also seen our own tragedies when some Irish homes were swallowed by fire. It is important that people in Britain pay heed to the political decisions that made the Grenfell Tower blaze possible, but it should also prompt Irish people to reflect on how we, as a society, have agreed to organise housing.

When a fire at a halting site in Carrickmines resulted in ten fatalities in 2015, local residents actually blockaded the area to stop building equipment from providing emergency housing on a nearby vacant plot. In the context of a homelessness crisis that continues to accelerate, when a former B&B in Clontarf was purchased to provide emergency accommodation for families without a place to live, local protests ensued.

What unites property owners in Kensington, Carrickmines, and Clontarf is prosperity. These are aspirational locations, neighbourhoods that come with a premium price. Everyone upset in Kensington about re-housing policies expressed their horror at the Grenfell tragedy. Those protesting in Carrickmines granted that 'you'd have to be sad for them' but those left behind after the blaze were 'not wanted here'. The residents in Clontarf were keen to express their 'sincere sympathy' for those who are without homes, but they still opposed the development. We are reminded of the skilled lawyer who famously asked Jesus, 'But who is my neighbour?'

Jesus' answer was to tell the parable of the Good Samaritan. 'Go and do likewise,' he teaches, after recounting the story of how mercy so often comes from unexpected places. The Grenfell Tower blaze was not a natural disaster, but a political one. In Scott Prather's theological examination of the aftermath of Katrina, he argues strongly that our planning systems are established to ensure that people at the top are protected from such tragedies. This is why it is insufficient to wash our hands by speaking in resigned tones of regulatory neglect. The arrangement that means that the cheapest materials go to public housing and the fire-services are stripped to the bone is not unintentional. It is with deliberate and considered care that these decisions are perpetually made. We care more about satisfying the markets than protecting people. The human cost in lives lost and homes ruined was the inevitable consequence of the British political commitment to austerity.

And it is on this level that the tragedy of Grenfell Tower relates to us in Ireland. As Dublin races into yet another bubble, our collective belief that property is a commodity is reflected across our government policy. We have largely stopped building public housing (Ruth Coppinger reports that only 253 units were completed last year). We provide social housing through structures that subsidise private landlords. We respond to homelessness with makeshift solutions. We allow international vulture funds to exacerbate the rental crisis. We can look on in disbelief as those with a lot resent the basic charity offered to those left with nothing after the Grenfell blaze, but the Irish housing system is riven by systemic inequalities that leave it as fragile. We do not have a good track record of offering hospitality to those who find themselves without a place to lay their head.

Hospitality is the heart of the Gospel. From Abraham welcoming the three strangers, in Genesis 18, right through to Mary's famous 'thy will be done', the entire narrative arc of the Bible rests on the everyday responsibility to care for whoever it is that God puts in our path. In Ireland, our politics of housing does the exact opposite. It leaves individuals to fend for themselves. It rewards and strengthens those who are already strong and rewarded. It takes an essential part of human life – a home – and leaves it to the vagaries of the market.

As we reflect on Grenfell Tower, praying for those

who are bereaved and supporting those who are left behind, we should also consider how we can care for the slow-motion tragedy afflicting our neighbours closer to home. Re-weaving the social fabric is the task set before us. Agitating for a return to providing high-quality social housing and enshrining housing as a human right would be two constructive steps we could take to avoid sounding like that skilled lawyer pretending not to know who his neighbour was.

7
Leonard Cohen, Resounding Hallelujah

The surname of this famous Canadian singer-songwriter – Cohen – actually means 'priest' in Hebrew. His favourite book was the Bible. And the word with which he'll always be associated is 'Hallelujah', a truly wonderful word, combining two Hebrew words, 'hallelu' (praise ye), and 'Yah' (the Lord). Hallelujah appears repeatedly in the Psalms and pops up again in the Book of Revelation. Despite only appearing in these two books of the Bible, it's a word that has touched countless people.

Leonard Cohen was never a happy-clappy type of singer. With deadpan humour, he made fun of his own reputation as 'the godfather of gloom' during a concert in London, in July 2008: 'It's been a long time since I stood on the stage in London. It was about 14 or 15 years ago. I was 60 years old, just a kid with a crazy dream. Since then I've taken a lot of Prozac, Paxil, Welbutrin, Effexor, Ritalin,

Focalin. I've also studied deeply the philosophies and religions, but cheerfulness kept breaking through'.

Leonard Cohen's song 'Hallelujah' stands out from a lot of contemporary pop: there is no aggressive drum beat or loud bass guitar to be heard. It sounds more like a waltz. And the message is not a lovey-dovey one. It's real, it's gritty, and it's ultimately about surrender, about letting go and letting God in. Before we're willing to surrender, we need to admit that we cannot do things on our own. Just like King David, the protagonist of the song 'Hallelujah', who, despite finding a hidden chord that pleased God, soon found his life going desperately out of tune after he saw Bathsheba bathing on the roof, took her to himself, made her pregnant and killed her husband, thus committing a much worse sin to hide his initial one.

Cohen's song quickly moves from King David to the legendary warrior Samson. His power left him when Delilah cut his long mane of hair. Two powerful men found their power and prestige unravelling at lightning speed. It's only when you fall into the dust and discover your brokenness that you're ready to see that you have next to nothing to offer God. But God can do everything with nothing, and that's why it's worth daring to stand before God 'with nothing on my tongue but Hallelujah'.

Even our holiest ideas can be mistaken: it's not the amount of money we give away, or the hours we spend in prayer that stand to us in the long run. What really makes the difference is love, our loving and confident surrender to God's dream for our lives. It's that marvellous moment of surrender that Cohen is hinting at when he explains the song Hallelujah with these tremendous words: 'regardless of what the impossibility of the situation is, there is a moment when you open your mouth and you throw open your arms and you embrace the thing and you just say "Hallelujah! Blessed is the name". And you can't reconcile it in any other way except in that position of total surrender, total affirmation'.

May Leonard Cohen rest in peace and rise with a resounding Hallelujah.

8

An IRA leader turned peacemaker

Tributes poured in from across the political divide when Martin McGuinness' death was announced on 21 March 2017, the date of the spring equinox. Martin's story is one of darkness and light, the darkness of how he and so many Catholic young nationalists found themselves imprisoned by lack of opportunity, prejudice and isolation from an occupying establishment. The Bogside was indeed a place of great challenge.

In the Bogside, Catholics were poor and oppressed, civil rights marches turned into riots and the British army was deployed on the streets. McGuinness was born to a Roman Catholic family in Derry in 1950. He became involved with the Republican movement at a young age. McGuinness believed armed struggle was the only way to achieve a free Derry. By 21, he was the second-in-command of the IRA in his home city – a position he held at the time of

Bloody Sunday in 1972. Bloody Sunday, which resulted in the deaths of 14 men and boys, bolstered support for the IRA and McGuinness. He quickly rose through the ranks of the Provisional IRA, as its campaign of violence targeted Unionists and Catholics who did not toe the line.

A divisive figure, he was pivotal in Northern Ireland's peace negotiations, ultimately choosing politics over violence. As the countless deaths continued, the IRA began to realise that the conflict was not going to end this by military means. A ceasefire was announced and negotiations began, resulting in The Good Friday Agreement.

Rev Harold Good, one of the independent witnesses overseeing the decommissioning of the IRA weaponry, said of him, '[H]ad he [McGuinness] not come from that place, he would not have been able to bring other people with him on that journey. That must not be forgotten. But McGuinness had a tough battle persuading republicans to decommission weapons and support policing and the rule of law, and the negotiators knew it'. Peter Hain, former secretary of state of Northern Ireland, said, 'At one point it got so heated that Gerry Adams and Martin McGuinness cornered me in a cupboard, in Hillsborough Castle, and really tried to threaten me. Threaten me that I would get sacked by Tony Blair the prime minister from my job. I knew it was nonsense. Eventually a deal was struck'. The DUP's Ian Paisley remembered, 'Doing a deal with that person was probably the most important arrangement we had to come to, because if we could do a deal with Martin McGuinness and we could work with Martin McGuinness, we could do a deal with any republican because he was the authentic voice'. Once bitter enemies, Ian Paisley Snr and McGuinness created a devolved government representing their sides as equals. A partnership, even friendship, developed, and they were dubbed the 'Chuckle Brothers'. His unlikely but genuine friendship with the late Ian Paisley was seen by many as symbolic of how far the North came after the Troubles, the three-decade period of conflict before the Good Friday Agreement was signed in 1998. Former US President Bill Clinton – who phoned the McGuinness family to express his condolences – tweeted that McGuinness was 'steadfast and courageous' in his pursuit for a 'shared future for Northern Ireland'.

In the UK, former government minister Norman Tebbit, whose wife was paralysed by an IRA bombing of a Brighton hotel in 1984, told ITV's *Good Morning Britain* that he hoped McGuinness was 'parked in a particularly hot and unpleasant corner of hell for the rest of eternity'. However, Jo Berry, whose father was killed in the same hotel, publically shared her compassionate hope in a peace process that McGuinness played such a massive role in.

As we welcome the longer and brighter days of spring, may we also always embrace the light of hope, reconciliation and new beginning. May the people of Northern Ireland continue to embrace diversity and be a living bridge of tolerance, acceptance and compassion. May Martin McGuinness, whose life longed for true justice, rest in peace.

Part 3
Where Church and society collide

9
Defending the Eighth Amendment

The Eighth Amendment to the Constitution is Ireland's original life equality amendment. Notwithstanding the abortion legislation of 2013, the Eighth Amendment provides the last remaining protection for the unborn child in Ireland and must be robustly defended. Each human being, regardless of age, gender, disability, race, or status in society, possesses a profound, inherent, equal and irreplaceable value and dignity. Abortion advocates want the unborn child to be an exception to this rule. To do this, they resort to the ploy of denying the humanity of the unborn. The sign of a truly civilised society, however, is one that welcomes *everyone* in life and protects *everyone* in its laws.

Minister Katherine Zappone believes that only offering abortions in cases of incest, rape and fatal foetal abnormality would 'do nothing at all for most women in Ireland'.

As a citizen of this republic, I am absolutely shocked and saddened that a minister with responsibility for children would be so vociferous in her determination to legislate for a liberal-style abortion on demand. Does her fundamental responsibly not extend itself to protecting the vulnerable life of unborn children in the womb? The minister's attitude is mirrored by a clear bias in national media for repealing the Eighth Amendment. This bias must be challenged. Our licence fees pay huge salaries to national broadcasters, who actively promote repealing the Eighth Amendment. This is also a national disgrace that goes unchallenged by the mainstream.

One of the fundamentals of our Constitution is supporting life, from the cradle to the grave, from the womb to the tomb. Children living in the womb must, as the Proclamation of the Irish Republic states, at 'all times be treasured'.

I am also deeply outraged that the same minister and government seem much less inclined to creating a culture of life and dignity for vulnerable children. I think of so many children living in hotel rooms because of homelessness. Families struggling to provide basic nutrition to children. I'm conscious of the huge cutbacks in terms of resources for children with special needs. The list is endless. And yet this minister calls for legislation to allow lives with wonderful potential and hope to be abruptly ended by abortion.

I am convinced that, despite a strong campaign to repeal the Eighth Amendment, natural orientation of the vast majority of citizens is pro-life. How many mothers and fathers come to believe in the miracle of life the first time they feel the flicker of life in the womb? My mother always said the greatest miracle is to hold her babies for the first time. How many parents greatly grieve the loss of life due to miscarriage and cherish every moment of their child's life in the womb? Being pro-life is part of our DNA. Our inclination is to live, as is that of a child in the womb.

Bring on a referendum as soon as possible. End this constant negative secular culture of death. Please, in the name of our humanity and our God, defend the dignity of unborn children living in the womb.

10

Vocation Crisis

We have no young priests. At 42 years of age, I am the youngest diocesan priest in Kildare-Leighlin. This is a rather overwhelming wake-up call to the Church. What about our witness seems to be so unattractive that it discourages other young men from entertaining the idea of priestly vocation? I remember mentioning vocation at a sixth-year graduation Mass and provoking laughter in the audience.

We fail to listen to young people's reasons why priestly vocation is not a viable option for them. We hope things will change but our leadership regrettably fails to imagine the necessary changes. Our bishops seem to forget the issues of priestly celibacy, the ordination of women and lay ministry, despite Pope Francis' call to be open, bold and real. The old model simply is no longer working. The Church is not dead but the model we work out of fundamentally needs to die. Our vocation crisis is currently a huge burden on elderly clergy because of extra duties. Keeping the show on the road or the ship floating is not what Christ calls us to do. Priestly celibacy simply makes no sense at all for many priests and lay people alike. I often listen to parents in church who tell me that under no circumstance is their son to enter the priesthood. Priests' lives are perceived as lonely, removed from reality and at best, strange. Why is the institutional Church digging its head in the sand and failing to recognise this fact?

In September 2015, 17 young men entered Maynooth to study for the priesthood, bringing the total number of clerical students in Ireland's only seminary for diocesan priests to 60. The figure, up a few on last year, has been hovering around the same mark for some years now. Considering that not all those who enter the seminary are ordained, the death rate of priests and the needs of parishes, it is clear that 17 doesn't even begin to address what everyone now accepts is a vocations crisis.

A new reality has dawned. Parishes are now effectively being amalgamated, though we resist using the word. Priests are not being replaced. Masses are being curtailed. Priests are disappearing in Ireland. Many priests who had reached the retirement age of 75 have agreed to soldier on, helping to temporarily camouflage an inevitable reality.

The latest initiative to solve the vocations crisis (or to push back the obvious solution for as long as possible) is to import priests from abroad. Already here and there, priests from overseas have served in Irish parishes, mainly Polish priests serving Polish communities, but also African and Indian priests. And now many dioceses have decided to establish a structured link with an Indian diocese so that some of their priests will be transferred to an Irish diocese and be given a number of parishes. It appears that the initiative is regarded as a pilot scheme that, if successful, might kick the celibacy can down the road a few years more. It is the last throw of the dice in an effort to avoid the inevitable. It seems fair and sensible to say that, if we brought the faith to other nations in past centuries, isn't it time for them to reciprocate? But it's not quite as simple as that. For one thing missioning in Africa or Asia a hundred years ago is different from missioning in Ireland now. The context is completely different. Priests are not like footballers that can be transferred for a given fee from Real Madrid to Manchester United. The size of the pitch and the width of the goal posts are the same in Madrid as in Manchester.

Priesting is different. Language matters. Culture matters. Tradition matters. History matters. Understanding is about more than knowing the words. Appreciating the weave and waft of Irish society is essential to ministering to people's needs at parish level. Even accent can be a bar to communication. Accent-wise, even a Cork priest working in a Derry diocese (or vice-versa) may present difficulties. It used to be said about Pope John Paul that he tried to replicate Polish

Catholicism throughout the world. And the problem with African or Indian priests, for example, is that they may try to replicate their own pastoral practices and thereby cause more problems than they will solve. For instance, if priests are used to not allowing laity to be involved in worship, how long will they survive in an Irish parish? If priests are used to not allowing women to be involved in parish life except in a peripheral and patronising way, how long will they survive in an Irish parish? They could empty our already-emptying churches in a decade.

As the Irish Catholic Church has an apparently flawless talent for getting things exactly wrong, we need to be careful. We need to re-think this new strategy through, before we find ourselves going down another cul-de-sac. Ultimately, we priests have the responsibility to accept how we have got to where we find ourselves today. Yes, we can blame the media, secular culture etc. But that defensive argument will not bring us to the truth. Many priests themselves are living in vocational crisis; they are disillusioned, downhearted, burnt-out and depressed. Over the past year, four priests I know have committed suicide. How many of us priests present an image of fulfilment, happiness and contentment? Many clergy heroically contribute to the lives of parish well into their eighties, which, though generous, merely keeps the ship floating and it sails at half-mast. There is a palpable sense of fatigue and apathy among clergy, in my experience.

Living on our comfortable salaries leads to a tendency of selfishness and even greed. There is a clear lack of fire in the belly, particularly among younger priests, who are often much more passionate about liturgical norms and clerical dress than the fundamental issues of social justice. How many younger priests are far more passionate about their time off parish duty than being on the ground missioning with the people of God? But we need to be available and attentive to the needs of the people we live with, present in our school communities, hospitals and in the general life of parish. I find ministry deeply relevant and necessary here in Portlaoise. It's wonderful to have a work base, a parish centre, a pulse where the community gathers and engages. This has brought me great joy and fulfillment. How many priests around the country have no proper workspace, a place to be present and feel accompanied by a vibrant community? No wonder so many priests feel isolated, alone and disconnected from their communities.

Priesthood is a sacred gift by God to a faith community. This gift needs a new imagining in our western world.

11

Direct Provision
No Place to Call Home

Direct provision is one of the cruellest systems in contemporary modern Ireland. We have, through the *Ryan Report*, rightly condemned our shameful history of failing to care for the most vulnerable within institutions. I believe that the direct provision centres will be similarly condemned by future generations of young Irish citizens. Here in Portlaoise, the direct provision centre, Montague Hotel, houses dozens of adults and children in a cramped, austere, depressing and bleak environment. Direct provision is a cynical response by successive governments to the refugee crisis. There is an in-built racism and xenophobia within Irish society. Often our holiest of folk feel free to condemn refugees. Direct provision never appeared on the agenda for the election in 2016. We adopt a counter-gospel attitude of 'Let them look after themselves'.

On 24 June 2014, the government indicated the continuance of the system of direct provision in its current form. The Minister for Justice Frances Fitzgerald noted:

'Direct provision is a system which facilitates the State providing a roof over the head of those seeking protection or on other grounds to be allowed to stay in the State. The Reception and Integration Agency (RIA) of my Department is responsible for the accommodation of protection applicants in accordance with the Government policy. I acknowledge that the length of time that residents spend in direct provision is an issue to be addressed. My immediate priority is that the factors which lead to delays in the processing of cases are dealt with so that protection seekers spend as little time as necessary in direct provision.'

Changes to the system of direct provision were indicated in the 'Statement of Government Priorities 2014-2016', where the following commitment was provided: 'While ensuring continued rigorous control of our borders and immigration procedures, we will treat asylum seekers with the humanity and respect they deserve. We are committed to addressing the current system of direct provision for asylum seekers to make it more respectful to the applicant and less costly to the taxpayer'. Junior Minister for Justice, Aodhán O' Ríordáin, acknowledged that 'direct provision needs radical reform. It is unacceptable that a child could spend half their life in a direct provision centre – in poverty, marginalised, stigmatised. I will be working closely with the Minister for Justice, Frances

Fitzgerald and officials on this. A lot of work has in fact already been done, and there is awareness within the department it has to change'.

Aodhán Ó Ríordáin often called personally to our local direct provision centre and made attempts to reform this corrupt system. His voice, however, was ignored by a government there to catch up in spinning recovery as opposed to engaging with citizens who never experienced this recovery. In the past, residents in the Montague Hotel have engaged with hunger strike because of the horror of their experience of direct provision. National media has covered this issue extensively. The Montague Hotel in Portlaoise houses over 60 children, many born and reared in this most restrictive and volatile environment. It's a dark story, that won't feature as a political issue, or concern most politicians or electors. It highlights our ability to hide the darker side of Irish society. Have we learnt anything from the past?

The Irish Refugee Council (IRC) is Ireland's only national non-governmental organisation to deal with refugees. The main work focus is on those in the asylum system who are applying to be recognised as refugees. For almost 20 years, the IRC have observed the changes that have been made in response to the arrival of refugees in Ireland. Based on extensive experience working directly with those affected, they have seen the huge financial cost of a failed system and the untold damage that has and is being done to men, women and children in the asylum process. Direct provision for asylum seekers in Ireland was introduced in 2000. It was originally envisaged that this system would accommodate people for no longer than six months. But there are now over 1,600 people who have spent five years or more living in centres. According to the Jesuit Refugee Service, 'there remains an unwavering need to advocate the cause of asylum seekers'.

According to David Moriarty, Policy and Advocacy Officer with JRS Ireland, much has changed in Ireland since 2000. But residents in direct provision face the same restrictions that were inherent in the system on day one. Asylum seekers are prohibited from taking up any form of employment. Instead, they receive a weekly cash allowance of €19.10 per adult and €15.60 per child. Meals are provided at set times in a common dining room as asylum seekers are not allowed to cook their own food. Parents of young children are still often allocated just one room for their entire family and they are forced to channel the most basic decisions relating to their children's welfare through the management of their accommodation centre.

Direct provision centres should be a reminder to all citizens of a brutal regime that alienates so many people from basic human rights.

12

Defending the integrity of Catholic schools

As Chaplain to a number of schools in Newbridge, Bagnelstown and Portlaoise, I have witnessed the life, energy, enthusiasm and rich diversity in our school communities. Catholic schools enjoy a rich tradition and continue, with an inclusive and holistic vision, to reach out to the diverse educational needs of our time. Catholic schools by their very nature are not exclusive clubs. Many different cultures, creeds and non-creeds coexist in a very progressive, inclusive and dynamic environment. A faith programme is part of the living ethos of Catholic schools and permeates every aspect of school curricula, not just the designated time allotted to more formal religious education. A positive sense of self – coupled with an image of God as a loving and compassionate friend, empowers young people to grow in self-confidence and develop a sense of justice and morality, which they will bring with them as they mature into active members of society.

I fundamentally disagree with the secular anti-Christian bias behind the attacks on our Catholic ethos. It is an agenda that I believe is led by a very small group of people and given a platform by the popular media. On the ground, parents are extremely happy with the excellent formation given in Catholic schools. Ruairi Quinn, a previous Minister of Education, suggested reducing the time allocated to teaching religion in schools. The Labour minister told an audience, at the Irish Primary Principals' Network annual conference, that 30 minutes of discretionary time for teaching religion could be reallocated to core subjects, to prioritise more 'important' curricular activities. I was appalled by these remarks. I find Quinn's secular bias and this discrimination against Catholic schools to be deeply worrying and indeed counter to the principle of religious freedom enshrined in our constitution. Mr Quinn's comments drew a speedy response from the Catholic bishops, who affirmed that Catholic schools provide for education of children while respecting the faith and treasured values of parents.

The suggestion to reduce teaching time for religious studies is unhelpful, unwarranted and unacceptable. It seems at best a hapless effort to devise educational policy 'on the hoof' and, at worst, an indication of an intention to undermine religious education in the vast majority of our schools. The minister initiated a consultation process on religious and cultural inclusion in primary schools. In

2011, religious institutions and the State commenced discussions to address how existing primary schools could address a more diverse range of faiths and no faith at all. In general, Irish parents want their children to receive an education in line with their own convictions. I value the Catholic ethos of schools and suggest that it enhances the lives of all its students.

Of course, in a pluralist society, the ethos of schools should reflect the various opinions of parents. I welcome the creation of non-faith based education centres. We should nonetheless recognise the huge debt of gratitude Ireland owes to the many religious organisations that upheld the nations' educational tradition. I am deliberate in my defence of Catholic schools and see a fundamental need to discover a moral, gospel-based pathway for our present and future generations. I am overwhelmed by young people's inspiration and honesty in discerning faith questions. Here in Portlaoise, there is an inspiring Sunday catechetical programme led by young students and their teacher from Scoil Chríost Rí. For fifteen years, the life and energy of principals and teachers who share the Good News have been such a positive witness. School communities are sacred places, microcosms of the enormous challenges and complexities of modern Ireland. They deserve support and investment as they work to create confident, ambitious and intelligent future leaders.

13
Sacramental preparation in Ireland

Pope Francis suggests that sacraments are not trophies for those who tick the right boxes. Sacraments should never be walls, with those who can receive on one side and those who don't meet regulations on the other. He prophetically presents an image of Church as a field hospital, a place where the most wounded find healing and comfort. Sacraments are not owned by anybody, they are that grace-filled bridge between our divine God and his human Church. In this regard, there is a responsibility to be available to the needs of our people. Sacraments provide strength and sustenance on our pathways through life. The Eucharist is life's greatest gift and food for the journey.

As a priest ministering in a busy parish, I am overwhelmed and often deflated by our casual understanding and lack of appreciation for this sacred gift. Every year I take a deep breath as I mentally prepare myself for the great effort involved in Baptism, Communion, Confirmation and marriage preparations. For many of the people involved, we merely provide the building and ritual for the big event. If not in a church, where could a bride walk up the aisle? There is a crisis of catechesis and an urgent need for renewal. The facts speak to this. 95 per cent of children who receive Confirmation do not attend church the following Sunday. Nourishing adult faith is the pathway to any real renewal of the Irish Church.

A tricky business

Hopefully, the occasions of Baptism, first Penance, first Communion, Confirmation and marriage are joyful ones, when families gather to celebrate and give thanks. The parish puts in a lot of effort and preparation for candidates. However, I increasingly find myself wondering what this experience is all about. Is it something that enriches the life of the parish community or does it highlight the huge disconnection between many families and regular sacramental worship?

Confirmation and Communion ceremonies can often be noisy gatherings. Most parishes have to police such occasions by constantly reminding those for whom a church is alien territory that the environment is a sacred and should evoke reverence. Texting, web browsing and a constant murmur suggests that for some, 'the sooner this is over, the better'. Stewards are often necessary to make sure conversation is kept to a minimum and smoking only takes place outside the church. This atmosphere is really regrettable and is particularly disappointing to the many families who do support and encourage their children to take the commitments they are making seriously. The commitment to become an active member of their respective faith communities is, of course, a huge task for any early adolescent candidate to Confirmation. But 'faith is caught, more so than taught'. If faith practice is not happening at home, it certainly will not happen to any Confirmation candidate, however warm the invitation from their local faith community. Now is the time to get real in how we prepare our young people for the sacraments. More than 95 per cent of parents here baptise their children, and 20 per cent practice their faith frequently. I am not making judgments about their decisions but I do question their authenticity. Might it be better for many families to have a baby party, a second-class party and a pre-teen right of passage party packed with bouncy castles, music and dance? Could they simply forget the Church altogether?

Young people are the future leaders of all our communities. Every day, I continue to be inspired by their enthusiasm, idealism and sense of justice. I love young people's sense of compassion. I often find them much more open to accepting difference than many adults. The Church needs to take the gift of its youth seriously. If we hand out a sacrament willy-nilly, it does not speak about the integrity and example that true catechesis encourage. It is not good enough and certainly not authentic to confirm a young person as a full member of the faith community and not see them again until they are presenting a child for Baptism or celebrating a marriage. In many European countries, Confirmation is not celebrated until late teens. In this way, young people remain connected and engaged with their local parish in a very real manner throughout the important transitional teenage years. An episcopal conference in South America has deferred Confirmation until much later so that candidates can truly embrace the full responsibility and gift of choosing, rather than receiving membership of a local parish. Could we take a break from the Sacrament of Confirmation for the next two years? A new vision and theology might better serve the faith development of our young people.

Part 4
Reflections and inspirations

14

The Year of Mercy

Pope Francis explained his decision to announce a Jubilee Year of Mercy in an interview with the Italian magazine *Credere*. 'I believe that this is the time for mercy', said the Pope. 'We are all sinners; all of us carry inner burdens'. According to the Holy Father, 'the world needs to discover that God is the Father, that there is mercy, that cruelty is not the way, that condemnation is not the way, because it is the Church herself who at times takes a hard line, and falls into the temptation to follow a hard line and to underline moral rules only; many people are excluded'. The Pope reminded us that everyone needs mercy, admitting, 'I still make mistakes and commit sins, and I confess every fifteen or twenty days'. The Jubilee Year might help the faithful to recognise 'the maternal dimension of God', observed the Pope. He explained that he was speaking of 'the tenderness, typical of a mother, God's tenderness that comes from his innate paternity. God is both father and mother'.

Mercy is indeed the great giver of life. Mercy is all about building bridges, not walls. Mercy is a divine gift that transcends the restrictiveness and limitations of our humanity. We often yearn for validation and encouragement, seeking it in places that often lead towards self-destruction. God's mercy is something radically different. None of us has to tick the right boxes in order to obtain God's gratuitous mercy, as we learn from the wonderful parable of the prodigal son.

The parable of the prodigal son

– Luke 15:11-32 (New International Version)
Jesus continued: 'There was a man who had two sons. The younger one said to his father, 'Father, give me my share of the estate'. So he divided his property between them.

'Not long after that, the younger son got together all he had, set off for a distant country and there squandered his wealth in wild living. After he had spent everything, there was a severe famine in that whole country, and he began to be in need.

'So he went and hired himself out to a citizen of that country, who sent him to his fields to feed pigs. He longed to fill his stomach with the pods that the pigs were eating, but no one gave him anything.

'When he came to his senses, he said, 'How many of my father's hired servants have food to spare, and here I am starving to death! I will set out and go back to my father and say to him: 'Father, I have sinned against heaven and against you. I am no longer worthy to be called your son; make me like one of your hired servants'. So he got up and went to his father.

'But while he was still a long way off, his father saw him and was filled with compassion for him; he ran to his son, threw his arms around him and kissed him.

'The son said to him, 'Father, I have sinned against heaven and against you. I am no longer worthy to be called your son'.

'But the father said to his servants, 'Quick! Bring the best robe and put it on him. Put a ring on his finger and sandals on his feet. Bring the fattened calf and kill it. Let's have a feast and celebrate. For this son of mine was dead and is alive again; he was lost and is found'. So they began to celebrate.

'Meanwhile, the older son was in the field. When he came near the house, he heard music and dancing. So he called one of the servants and asked him what was going on. 'Your brother has come', he replied, 'and your father has killed the fattened calf because he has him back safe and sound'.

'The older brother became angry and refused to go in. So his father went out and pleaded him. But he answered his father, 'Look! All these years I've been slaving for you and never disobeyed your orders. Yet, you never gave me even a young goat so I could celebrate with my friends.

But when this son of yours, who has squandered your property with prostitutes, comes home, you kill the fattened calf for him!'

"'My son', the father said, 'you are always with me, and everything I have is yours. But we had to celebrate and be glad, because this brother of yours was dead and is alive again; he was lost and is found".

This parable is the blueprint for Christian living. I often think that the loving father who went out to embrace his wayward son was prompted to do so by his wife. If any of my brothers or sister did not return by the agreed curfew time, my mother would insist that my father go out and find us. When he did find us, his greeting was not as warm as that of the father in the Gospel. Here in Portlaoise, I see mercy personified in the people who visit their children or partners in prison, reminding the prisoner that they are not alone and that love is greater than their crime. The Kingdom of mercy is full of doors that are opened, and in this regard I think especially of families who keep the door open to an often volatile and vulnerable family member.

The Kingdom of mercy also speaks the language of encouragement. The loving father in the parable didn't look for an inventory of his son's past sins. I believe that our merciful God has no memory of our past sins and that in this present moment his mercy resides in the depths of our heart; it is a gentle pulse telling us that we are loved, not for whom we may want to be, but for whom we really are. Ours is a merciful God, a God of acceptance, a God of empathy and a God whose mercy reaches for the most wounded places of our lives.

Some time ago, I was visiting a young father in a Portlaoise hospital. He was dying from pancreatic cancer. His partner kept vigil. The room had a spare bed. I suggested that she sleep for a while. 'Fr Paddy', she replied, 'what if he wakes up? He will not see me'. This is the merciful love of our Father in Heaven, a presence that never falls asleep, but intuitively awakens within us at our most vulnerable moments and gives us a sense that 'this too will pass'.

The year of mercy was a great gift for me. It's exactly what our Church should be constantly engaged with. A new theology and pastoral outreach through the Sacrament of Reconciliation is necessary. How many Confession boxes are just relics of yesterday's Church? Yes, people want a space and ritual for reconciliation, but the old formula is truly dying. Confession for children, for instance, is awkward and fundamentally needs a new vision and renewal. Mercy is also about action. As always, my inner consciousness niggles when we speak of mercy and fail to be compassionate in responding to the poorest of the poor. The Dublin archdiocese could, for example, take the radical step of donating Clonliffe and its land for affordable social housing in the heart of the city. Where are the voices of our hierarchy and Church leadership when it comes to real mercy issues? A more radical, merciful voice is needed. 'The voice crying in the wilderness prepares the way of the Lord' is very difficult to hear. Prophets like Peter McVerry, Brother Kevin and Sister Stan speak through their witness. The year of mercy was a call to get our hands dirty in the service of the Lord.

Mercy is easy when it comes to reciting certain prayers in order to avail of a spiritual reward. Mercy is much more challenging when it confronts our attitudes and our prejudice. Gossip is the antithesis of mercy. Deliberately putting others down is not the call of the true Christian. How many of us have suffered because of that idle comment or nasty word? Mercy is much more than kneeling at an altar. It's a mindset and way of life that liberates, encourages and offers us the opportunity to begin again every day. As St Augustine said, every saint has a past and every sinner has a future.

15
Christmas

In my own home, Christmas was the only time of the year when my father never drank. As a child, I loved him much more when he was sober. There were no arguments or tension in our home. My dad was a wonderful cook, a gift I have inherited from him. His specialties were stuffing and trifle. Despite a tight budget, my parents would go all out. On Christmas morning, it would be our father who would bring us down the stairs to see our stockings hanging on the banisters full of toffee sweets. When my father opened the sitting room door, we were greeted by the smell of the fresh pine Christmas tree. There were always gifts, gifts well beyond what my family could afford; there were bicycles and guitars. The Christmas turkey was also a great treat. Christ, the reason for this season, was to the fore of our attention. Masses in the cathedral in Carlow and visits to the cribs around the local churches are dear memories. Subconsciously, I was greatly attracted to the image of that family so poor and fragile and yet rich in humanity and love. I never really got into the more material aspect of the winter holiday.

Christmas is such a wonderful time of year. It is also a challenging time, particularly for those who experience bereavement, addiction, separation, financial or emotional concerns. Jesus is the God of the disenfranchised, the God of those who have not and long for something more. It's wonderful that poor shepherds tending their sheep were invited to be the first to see the Christ child, whose presence among us is as real today as it was over 2000 years ago. If Jesus was to be born again, he may well be born in a direct provision centre or one of the hostels that nearly 3000 children call home. There is no room at the inn for many people in Irish society. We have a very cosy and comfortable interpretation of the Jesus with whom we are presented in the liturgy. The radical vision and implication of incarnation fails to be truly communicated. The love of Christmas is felt more by those who have not than by those who have.

A story that has endured

For two millennia, people have told of the child in a Bethlehem manger, of the angels who announced his birth to shepherds and of learned men who travelled a great distance to see him. That a story persists for many years does not prove its truthfulness. Santa Claus, the Easter Bunny and the Tooth Fairy survive in the popular imagination. But a twenty-century tenure at least merits our consideration. What deep human longings does the Christmas story portray? Why has it connected so profoundly with millions of people? Is the story factual? Curiosity prompts further investigation.

A story of hope and survival

Jesus' society knew great pain and oppression. Rome ruled. Corrupt tax collectors burdened the people. Some religious leaders even sanctioned physical beating of Jewish citizens participating in compulsory religious duties.

Joseph and his pregnant wife Mary travelled a long distance to Bethlehem to register for a census but could not obtain proper lodging. Mary bore her baby and laid him in a manger, a feeding trough for animals. Eventually, King Herod sought to kill the baby. Warned of impending risk, Joseph and Mary fled to Egypt and then returned home after Herod's death. Imagine how Mary felt. Travelling while pregnant would be challenging. Fleeing to another land lest some king slay your son would not be pleasant. Yet she, Joseph, and Jesus survived the ordeal. In the midst of social and cultural challenges, the Christmas story offers encouragement and the hope of a new life linked to something – someone – greater than oneself.

A story of family

Christmas is a time for family gatherings. This interaction can bring great joy or great stress. Estrangement or ill-will from past conflicts can explode.

Joseph and Mary had their share of family challenges. Consider their circumstances. Joseph's fiancée became pregnant though she was a virgin. Mary believed the angel who told her that she was pregnant by God. Now, how would you feel if your fiancée exhibited evidence of sexual activity with someone else during your engagement? Suppose she said that God had sanctioned the whole thing. Would your trust and self-esteem take a nosedive? Would you cancel the wedding?

Joseph is described as a just man: 'Because Joseph her husband was faithful to the law, and yet did not want to expose her to public disgrace, he had in mind to divorce her quietly'. But an angel appeared to him in a dream, explaining that the child was conceived in her by God, and told him, 'you are to give him the name Jesus because he will save his people from their sins'. Joseph followed these instructions and cared for his family. His continuing commitment to Mary and Jesus played a significant part in the boy's birth and early childhood. With God's help, the family overcame major obstacles.

A story of love

Jesus' conception and birth were part of a divine plan to bring us genuine peace, inner freedom, and self-respect. God wants us to enjoy friendship with him, meaning and purpose. Alas, our own self-centredness separates us from him. Jesus came to bring us to God. Mary's baby was born to die, paying the penalty for our self-centredness. When the adult Jesus died on the cross, He paid for all our sins then rose from the dead to give new life.

Jesus explained, 'For God so loved the world that he gave his one and only Son, that whoever believes in Him shall not perish but have eternal life'. God can become your friend if you believe in him, that is, if you trust him to forgive you. He will never let you down.

Perhaps you are becoming aware of the importance of the Christmas story in your own life. Might you like to receive Jesus' free gift of forgiveness and place your faith in Him? You can celebrate this Christmas knowing that you are a member of His family. Perhaps you'd like to talk to Him right now. You might want to tell Him something like this:

Jesus Christ,
Thanks for loving me, for dying for my sins and rising again.
Please apply your death as the means of my forgiveness.
I accept your pardon.
Come and live in me and help me to become your close friend.

If you made the decision to place your trust in Jesus, he has entered your life, forgiven you and given you eternal life. I encourage you to tell someone about your decision and ask him or her to help you grow in faith. Read the Bible to discover more about God. Begin with the Gospel of John, the fourth book in the New Testament, which is one of the easier ones to understand. Tell God what is on your heart, and tell others about the discovery you've made so they can know Him too.

Christmas is meant to celebrate peace and joy. Amidst the business of shopping, remember that the Prince of peace came to spread peace and joy to all who believe in a light brighter than any winter darkness.

The story of Poinsettia

Poinsettia, a poor Mexican girl, had no gift to present to the baby Jesus in his crib as was customary on Christmas Eve. As Poinsettia walked slowly to the chapel with her friends and family, her heart was full of sadness rather than joy. An angel appeared to the little girl and told her, 'I am sure that even the most humble gift, if given in love, will be acceptable in his eyes'.

Not knowing what to do, the little girl knelt at the roadside and gathered a handful of common weeds, fashioning them into a small bouquet. Looking at these insignificant weeds, she felt more saddened and embarrassed than ever by the humbleness of her offering. Poinsettia fought back a tear as she entered the small village chapel. As she approached the crib she remembered the angel's words.

She felt her spirit lift as she knelt to lay the bouquet at the feet of the nativity scene. Suddenly, the bouquet of weeds burst into blooms of brilliant crimson red. All who saw it were certain that they had seen a miracle right before their eyes. From that day on, the bright red flowers were known as the *flores de buena*, or poinsettia to us.

The poinsettia offers us hope. Christmas is a time of cleansing, a time for renewal, a time for change. Jesus, born in great poverty to a family on the margins, is our source of new life, renewal, hope and confidence. Jesus feels our immense pain and suffering and dwells in our sometimes-disillusioned hearts.

The gift of Christmas is a bright light that is so much brighter than any darkness. There is no recession when it comes to the Kingdom of Jesus Christ. There are no cutbacks in the unconditional love Jesus has for us all. The new life of Jesus Christ is not something that just happened once, but a promise that is to be realised in all our lives. This is the time. It is the weeds of hurt and brokenness, disillusionment and anger that we place at the foot of our saviour this Christmas. His presence will transform and allow us to begin again.

16

It's OK not to be OK

For fifteen years, I have ministered to an open wound in Irish society: death by suicide. These are tragic deaths that bring a deep sense of loss to the broken hearts of loved ones. Vibrant and talented young lives tragically come to an abrupt and devastating end. Words are so inadequate in times of such tragedy, which leaves parents and families with wounds that may never be fully healed. Unanswered questions intensify their pain.

At times in our lives it's Ok not to be OK. We are fragile people who feel the wounds and scars of our humanity. Help and support is available if we need to share our pain at vulnerable moments in our life. To ask for help requires courage but guarantees a path to recovery and healing.

Before his death, Donal Walsh, the Kerry teenager whose battle with cancer touched so many lives, implored his peers to value life. In his anti-suicide video, which was distributed to every secondary school in the country, he said, 'I realised that I was fighting for my life for the third time in four years and this time I have no hope. Yet still I hear of young people committing suicide and I'm sorry but it makes me feel nothing but anger. I feel angry that these people choose to take their lives, to ruin their families and to leave behind a mess that no one can clean up'. He pleaded, 'Please, as a 16-year-old who has no say in his death sentence, who has no choice in the pain he is about to cause, and who would take any chance at even a few more months on this planet: appreciate what you have, know that there are always other options and help is always there'.

'Suicide is a permanent solution to a temporary problem', he affirms. It leaves a permanent heartache in the lives of loved ones who are left wounded, bereaved, broken, and still wondering why a sibling, son or daughter, partner, neighbour, or friend would end their life in such a tragic manner. Of course the darkness and despair in those final moments of a life ended by suicide in no way define the totality of that person's life. 'Nothing can separate us from the love of God'. God's love is best summed in the words of our dying saviour on the cross: 'Today you will be with me in paradise'.

Suicide is an alarming reminder of how fragile and vulnerable the human mind is. I believe mental illness is the most difficult human cross to carry. When illness is physically manifested, it is tangible, acceptable and real. Illness of the mind is subtler and less apparent than a broken leg or physical illness. Mental illness can be hidden, stigmatized and much more difficult to 'fix'. Perhaps the greatest devastation that results from suicide is the unanswered questions that loved ones will forever struggle with. Why did this happen? Should I have recognised the signs? How did I not know that they were so unhappy?

The burdens, anxiety and overwhelming despair that bring somebody to end their own life must be the loneliest and most vulnerable crosses any human has to carry. I suggest that theirs surely is the Kingdom of Heaven, a kingdom that transforms despair into hope, darkness into light, and being lost into the joy of being found. Any individual whose life has ended in the darkness of suicide also has a life story filled with brightness, gentleness and tremendous actions of human love. In dark difficult days of uncertainty, please talk to somebody. Take advantage of the many listening ears that can offer support and help. It's OK not to be OK.

17
Exam time

One of the great connections I have in every secondary school is with Leaving Cert students. The Leaving Cert is an important exam but must never totally define a young person's life. Cutbacks to counselling and career guidance in our secondary schools have left a huge deficit. It is a competitive age and young people should never judge themselves according to the amount of points they achieve in the state exam. My strong desire for young people is to find a pathway where personal fulfilment and growth will allow them to blossom in their adult lives.

The Leaving Certificate is an important milestone in the lives of our young people. This is an anxious time for students. It is also a time for us all to encourage and support, a time when our spirituality can make young people gain a confidence that will inspire hope. Being open to the love of God in our lives is a great gift. Saint Paul said,

'With God on our side, who can be against us'. It is challenging to be a young person today, with the competitive environment that is the point's race, the struggle to find the right college course and career path, and the uncertain global economy in which so often only the fittest and leanest survive. There is little room for failure in our culture. We have become hard on each other – as this young generation have been in terms of bullying, peer pressure, prejudice and exclusion.

I understand why Leaving Cert students often find themselves engaging in school liturgies and lighting candles in their local church. Faith in the living God is a great source of strength and love for our young friends. Yes, there will always be difficulty and disappointment in life, but faith gives us a confidence and inner peace that allows us all to live life to the full. God invites us to manifest our hopes and dreams into the realities of our day-to-day lives. Faith is grounded in the knowledge that our God abundantly loves us for who we are, not for who we try to be. Faith allows us to hope even in the face of adversity and human struggle.

Faith tells us that we are not alone. Our God resides in the depths of our human experience, even in the stress of getting ready for the Leaving Certificate. A prayer I always contemplated as I faced exam time and never let me down was:

Holy Spirit,
Send your power,
Help me to remember all that I have learnt,
Inspire me with the gift of knowledge,
Amen.

18
Bereavement: a difficult pathway

During the rite of ordination, a bishop says the following words to the priest, 'Model your life on the mystery of the Lord's cross'. The cross is not just a symbol of suffering and Christ's solidarity with those who are vulnerable but it is also a hope-filled statement that God's light is so much more radiant than the shadows of our wounds. Priesthood is inextricably linked to the crosses and wounds of society. One of those huge wounds I minister to day in, day out is the reality of death and bereavement. Hopefully I will never turn into a robot and minister to these situations in a detached and clinical manner. I also hope that I won't become so engaged as to become overwhelmed. Empathy is the ability to feel another's emotions as if they were your own.

For me to minister well in funerals and bereavements, I must also be aware of my own grief story. Though relatively young, I have already lost both my parents and my brother Jimmy. My mother's loss was very difficult.

She died after a long battle with breast cancer, a terrible rollercoaster of chemotherapy, remission and the eventual terminal diagnosis. Her suffering was immense. Ministering to your own family is very different. At the thought of being without her, I became like a little child; I was frightened and silenced. It reminded me of my uncle Jack at his mother's deathbed. She was 99 and Jack was 74. At the end, he roared, 'Don't leave me, Mammy!' Days before my mammy died I celebrated Mass with all my family around my mother's bed. I had not even been ordained for a year. It was the most difficult Mass I ever celebrated, lots of tears and yet a powerful sense of God's gentle presence calling us to be strong and at peace. I will never forget my mother's words to those gathered around her bed, the same bed we often jumped into as children, feeling so loved and cared for. She said: 'I have total peace and serenity' and 'miss me but let me go'.

Miss me but let me go
When I come to the end of the road
And the sun has set on me,
I want no rites in a gloom-filled room,
Why cry for a soul set free.
Miss me a little – but not too long,
And not with your head bowed low,
Remember the love that we once shared,
Miss me – but let me go.

For this is a journey that we all must take,
And each must go alone.
It's all a part of the master's plan,
A step on the road to home.
When you are lonely and sick of heart,
Go to the friends we know.
And bury your sorrows in doing good deeds,
Miss me – but let me go.

My dad's death, difficult as it was, carried a sense of consolation for me. I knew that he was reunited with the love of his life. Part of him died when our mother died. He became somewhat reclusive, withdrawn and unable to cope. After his own diagnosis, he lasted four weeks. As he died, he also revealed his deep faith. In his final few years, I had formed a comfortable relationship with him. While serving in Bagnelstown in Co. Carlow, I could drive in to visit him. We would sit in the sitting room, often looking at a movie. In his silence I felt very comfortable. I'm gratefully aware of how much my brother Noel cared for our father. Noel possesses a remarkable innate kindness, which I greatly value.

My eldest brother Jimmy died tragically at the young age of 42. Jimmy also carried the cross of addiction. The only person he really harmed because of this was himself. He was loved by many but never discovered the pathway of recovery. Tragically, he fell down the stairs in his home and was found dead on a Sunday afternoon by my sister Esther. I was en route to visit him with a lemon cake. When my sister phoned, I intuitively knew that something was wrong. As any sibling of an addict can understand, Jimmy was always a cause of worry. So many opportunities and invitations were given to my beloved brother but he was not in a space to accept.

A Garda was called and came up to talk to me. He remembered me from a similar situation I had been called to just two days prior. 'You're here again', he said. 'Yes', I answered, 'but this time it's my brother'. I think I repressed the loss and jumped straight into the role of priest, celebrating my brother's Mass with a great sense of disbelief. His loss is a private one for me, one that is still difficult to carry; his memory is so very close to my heart.

I think it's very important to publicly share my grief story because it's something that everyone has. It's part of who we are. When we fail to tend to our grief, we can do huge damage to our psychological well-being. The more we visit our grief, the more we can live with it. We never fully get over a loss nor perhaps are we called to; all we can do is live with it.

Remembering

Death is that challenging confrontation that reminds us that 'we are only here for a short time'. Death is difficult and painful. It strips us of the familiar and often leaves us naked and vulnerable. The death of a loved one often leaves many unanswered questions as we attempt to carry on without a husband or wife, sibling or friend.

Perhaps the two most powerful lines in the entire gospel describe the human emotion felt by Jesus when his friend Lazarus died. 'Jesus wept'. Jesus knew the pain and hurt that comes when a loved one dies. And for God to fully embrace the human condition, he also had to embrace death through his Son. The humiliating and brutal manner of Christ's death united God with all types of suffering and persecution. The words that came from our dying God were a prayer of welcome and wonderful invitation: 'Today, you will be with me in paradise'.

We know from our experience that the leaves will blossom again, that spring will come. Christ's death was the ultimate demonstration of love by his father. As he was awoken to new life and resurrection, so too are all who believe in Him. As we remember our loved ones who have died and as we pray for them, we do so with great hope in our hearts. Saint Paul tells us that 'our true home is in heaven'. May all our loved ones enjoy the eternal promise of life and peace in the happiness and joy of God's presence. Jesus tells us, 'I am going ahead of you to prepare a place for you, so that where I am, you, too, shall be'. And despite the pain that comes when a loved one dies, in faith we are encouraged to hope in the fact that God's love is even brighter than death itself.

Pádraig Pearse once told a beautiful story to demonstrate our Christian hope regarding death.

In the month of September, the little boy asked his mother where all the swallows went. 'To the land where it is always summer'.

A Prophet of hope to a wounded people

Sister Consilio received an MBE in 2011 for her heroic commitment to good people who live with serious addiction. In the early 1980s, she established a Cuan Mhuire Community in Newry, similar to her well-known Rehabilitation Centre in Athy. A humble and deeply spiritual woman, Sister Consilio once remarked, 'a life recovering from addiction is a life worth living'.

Consillio's life has helped thousands of people who find themselves surrounded by the darkness and despair of being lost in and imprisoned to addiction. Many of these people have suffered huge losses in terms of their personal dignity, professional lives, marriages, families and friendships. Addiction to alcohol and harmful substances is a very true reality in all our communities. Ireland unfortunately has one of the highest percentages of alcohol addiction in the world. Consillio's philosophy emphasises the importance of the individual's personal story. Addiction not only affects the addict but also the entire family. It is a dark and deadly disease that truly can destroy lives.

Frances Black, founder of the RISE foundation, courageously shared her personal story at our annual novena. She became enslaved to alcohol. Her darkness brought her to a place of misery and inner turmoil. As she spoke that night, hundreds of people in a packed congregation could relate her story to that of a family member or relative in a similar circumstance. One young man embraced a radical, positive new beginning that night. Perhaps with God's grace, he made a promise that he would never drink alcohol again. Eight months later, he enjoys a whole new quality of life, emotionally, physically and spiritually. He enjoys a much more fulfilling and happy lifestyle. This young man is typical of the thousands of people who have been healed through the rehabilitation process directed by real life heroes such as Sister Consilio.

Recovery from addiction is about embracing powerlessness. Many parents, siblings and partners are greatly affected by alcohol abuse. A great therapist once said 'we are only as sick as our best kept secret'. Recovery is always a possibility. We are all in need of healing. Recovery from addiction is gradual, worthwhile and very necessary for thousands of people whose lives sink daily into a pit of darkness and despair. The unsung heroes of recovery place their trust in a higher power, a source of inspiration and tremendous peace, a reservoir of real healing that quenches the thirst of any addiction.

In his book *The Wounded Healer*, Henri Nouwen

embraces his vulnerable self and in doing so, finds empathy and love in his rich life of service to people who are bruised and broken. In a hopeful and uplifting attitude he says, 'Often our scars and wounds can be our greatest gift, it allows us to share the cross with one another'. For all who carry the cross of addiction, the Serenity Prayer is most appropriate.

God grant me the serenity
To accept the things I cannot change;
Courage to change the things I can;
And wisdom to know the difference.

Living one day at a time;
Enjoying one moment at a time;
Accepting hardships as the pathway to peace;
Taking, as He did, this sinful world
As it is, not as I would have it;
Trusting that He will make all things right
If I surrender to His Will;
That I may be reasonably happy in this life
And supremely happy with Him
Forever in the next.
Amen.

Part 5
Parables and prayers

19

Stories and prayers

The mouse in the house

The following story is a simple but gentle reminder that we all have an important role to play in life.

A mouse looked through the crack in the wall to see the farmer and his wife open a package. What food might it contain, the mouse wondered. When they opened it, he was devastated to discover it was a mousetrap. Retreating to the farmyard, the mouse cried, 'There is a mousetrap in the house! There is a mousetrap in the house!'

The chicken clucked and scratched, raised her head and said, 'Mr Mouse, I can tell this is a grave concern to you, but it is of no consequence to me. I cannot be bothered by it'.

The mouse turned to the pig and told him, 'There is a mousetrap in the house'. The pig sympathised but said, 'I am so very sorry, Mr Mouse, but there is nothing I can do about it but pray. Be assured you are in my prayers'.

The mouse turned to the cow and said, 'There is a mousetrap in the house!' The cow said, 'Wow, Mr Mouse. I'm sorry for you, but it's no skin off my nose'.

So, the mouse returned to the house, dejected, to face the farmer's mousetrap alone. That very night a sound was heard throughout the house – the sound of a mousetrap catching its prey. The farmer's wife rushed to see what was caught. In the darkness, she did not see that it was the tail of a venomous snake. The snake bit the farmer's wife. The farmer rushed her to the hospital, and she returned home with a fever.

Everyone knows you treat a fever with fresh chicken soup, so the farmer took his hatchet to the farmyard for the soup's main ingredient. But his wife's sickness continued, so friends and neighbours came to sit with her around the clock. To feed them, the farmer butchered the pig. The farmer's wife died. So many people came for her funeral that the farmer had the cow slaughtered to provide enough meat for all of them. The mouse looked upon it all with great sadness from his crack in the wall.

The next time you hear that someone is facing a problem and think it doesn't concern you, remember the mouse in the house.

Story of Appreciation

A young academically excellent person applied for a managerial position in a big company. He passed the first interview. The director did the last interview and would make the last decision. The director discovered from his CV that the youth's academic achievements were excellent all the way, from secondary school until postgraduate research, never did he have a year when he did not score highest marks.

The director asked, 'Did you obtain any scholarships in school?'

'None'.

'Was it your father who paid your school fees?'

'My father passed away when I was one year old, it was my mother who paid all my school fees.'

'Where did your mother work?'

'My mother works as a washer of clothes.'

The director requested the youth to show his hands. The youth showed a pair of hands that were smooth and perfect.

'Have you ever helped your mother wash clothes?'

'Never, my mother always wanted me to study and read more books. Furthermore, my mother can wash clothes faster than me.'

'I have a request. When you go back home today, go and clean your mother's hands, and then see me tomorrow morning.'

The youth felt that his chance of landing the job was high. When he went back home, he happily requested that his mother let him clean her hands. His mother felt strange, happy but with mixed feelings. She showed her hands to her son. The youth cleaned his mother's hands slowly. Tears fell as he did. It was the first time he noticed that his mother's hands were so wrinkled and full of cuts and bruises. Some bruises were so painful that his mother shivered when they were cleaned with water. This was the first time the youth realised that it was this pair of hands washing other people's clothes every day that had enabled him to pay his school fees. The bruises in his mother's hands were the price she paid for his graduation, academic excellence and future. After cleaning his mother's hands, the youth quietly washed all the remaining clothes for his mother. That night, mother and son talked for a very long time.

Next morning, the youth went to the director's office.

The director, noticing the tears in the youth's eyes, asked, 'What did you do and learn yesterday?'

'I cleaned my mother's hands and also washed all the remaining clothes.'

'Please tell me what you felt.'

'I know now what appreciation is. Without my mother, there would be no successful me today. Also, by working together and helping my mother, I now realise how difficult and tough it is to get something done. Finally, I have come to appreciate the importance and value of family relationships.'

'This is what I am looking in my manager. I want to recruit a person who can appreciate the help of others, a person who knows the sacrifices involved in getting things done and a person who doesn't consider money his only goal in life. You are hired.'

Later on, this young person worked very hard and received the respect of his subordinates. Every employee worked diligently and as a team. The company grew from strength to strength.

The cracked pot

Life is a sacred journey.

A water bearer in India had two large pots. Each hung on the ends of a pole that he carried across his neck. One of the pots had a crack in it and was only ever half full, while the other pot was perfect and always delivered a full portion of water.

The water bearer worked like this for two years, delivering only one and a half pots of water to his house.

Of course, the perfect pot was proud of its accomplishments, of being perfect for the task for which it was made. But the poor cracked pot was ashamed of its own imperfection and its inability to accomplish what it had been made to do.

After two years of what it perceived to be a bitter failure, it spoke to the water bearer one day by the stream.

'I am ashamed of myself and I want to apologise to you. I have been able to deliver only half of my load because this crack in my side causes water to leak out all the way to your house. Because of my flaws, you have to do all of this work, and you don't get the full value from your efforts.'

The bearer said to the pot, 'Did you notice that there were flowers on your side of the path but not on the other pot's side? That's because I have always known about your flaw, and I planted flower seeds on your side of the path. Every day while we walk back, you watered them. For two years, I have been able to pick these beautiful flowers to decorate the table. Without you being just the way you are, there would not be this beauty to grace the house.'

Fragility is a most wonderful human trait. We are all broken and cracked – there is no use in denying it. Let us be cautious of our glorifying tendencies. This 'Wow, look at me' culture needs to stop once and for all. No more celebrating the most talented man or woman in the room. When we were younger, we needed lots of positive feedback, someone to say, 'You are a great boy at riding the bicycle'. As we grow older, we let go of the need to build ourselves up. We become aware of the need for accepting our strengths and weaknesses. Let us now say to each other: 'Wow, I am broken just like you'. People can surprise us when they are brave enough to be raw and open. They can jump in and share their own powerful fragility. This simple prayer is inspired by the cracked pots (that is, all of us!).

Dear God,
I'm quirky I know.
I don't always do things in the traditional way.
But I know what's right.
I know how to stand my ground for what I believe to be true.
Still, I need Your help, dear God.
You planted the seed.
You nourish me.
Shelter me now from the elements that stand in my way.
Help me grow.
Amen

A time to hope and plant

Nature so often reflects our human journey, and being in touch with Mother Earth helps us to be grounded and at one with our creator God. Life begins with the vibrancy of youth at springtime, maturing to restful summer calm, producing a rich harvest in autumn and indeed letting go to something new in winter.

Those of us who are lucky enough to have a garden perhaps have spent time tending to the needs of plants and shrubs. The garden is a fascinating place where life abounds. As we place our hands into the soil, we feel in many ways the pulse that beats from the heart that is

Mother Earth. It is uplifting for the soul to plant something small into the earth that with care and nourishment will grow and transform into something beautiful and unique. A colourful vibrant garden does not happen by accident, rather it is the result of hard work and great care in pruning, weeding, watering and nurturing. It is lovely to see so many gardens looking bright and cheerful.

We are all invited to plant at some time in our lives. God our Creator has invested and indeed planted so many gifts and talents into the depths of our being. This seed of potential grows in an environment of love, acceptance, hospitality and inclusion. When we don't realise the many gifts that we all have been blessed with, fear, resentment, hurt and judgment instead create a place of poverty where what was planted will die and wither.

Even if we have never planted a shrub or mowed a lawn, we are all called to be planters on our journey through life. Life connects us to each other; we cannot live in isolation, we are social beings. We must all care for the seeds of potential that are planted in our hearts. Where hospitality and welcome live, so too do growth and fulfilment. Warm greetings, a friendly smile, a cup of tea with a neighbour or friend provide that watering and nourishment that allow us to grow and blossom. This is necessary for young people especially.

The early stage after planting is the most vulnerable and because of this, it is also the time when most care and attention is necessary. Family life is the fundamental place of nurturing and encouragement. It is in the context of our family life that we discover and learn most. I often think about the huge task and responsibility of being a parent, the primary source of care and love for the young. Parenting requires generosity, selflessness and unconditional love.

I pray for all parents:

That the Lord will give you the health and strength that is necessary, as you tend to and nurture the treasures who live within your family garden.

May all of us take time some time to plant this summer, not just in our gardens but in our words of compassion and gentleness.

Inspiration of the praying hands

Back in the fifteenth century, in a tiny village near Nuremberg, lived a family with eighteen children. Eighteen!

In order to keep food on the table for this big family, the father and head of the household, a goldsmith by profession, worked almost eighteen hours a day at his trade and any other paying chore he could find in the neighbourhood. Despite their seemingly hopeless condition, two of Albrecht Dürer the Elder's children had a dream. They both wanted to pursue their talent for art but they knew full well that their father would never be financially able to send either of them to Nuremberg to study at the academy.

After many long discussions at night in their crowded

bed, the two boys finally worked out a pact. They would toss a coin. The loser would go down into the nearby mines and, with his earnings, support his brother while he attended the academy. Then, when that brother who won the toss completed his studies in four years, he would support the other brother at the academy, either through his art or through labouring in the mines.

They tossed a coin on a Sunday morning after church. Albrecht Dürer won the toss and went off to Nuremberg. Albert, the other brother, went down into the dangerous mines and for the next four years financed his brother, whose work at the academy was almost an immediate sensation. Albrecht's etchings, his woodcuts and his oils were far better than those of most of his professors, and by the time he graduated, he was beginning to earn considerable fees for his commissioned works.

When the now accomplished young artist returned home, the Dürer family held a celebration. Albrecht wanted to embrace his brother and allow him now to pursue his dream. Sadly Albert began to weep. He rose and wiped the tears from his cheeks.

'No, brother, I cannot go to Nuremberg. It is too late for me. Look at what four years in the mines have done to my hands! The bones in every finger have been smashed at least once and lately I have been suffering from such bad arthritis in my right hand that I cannot even hold a glass for your toast, much less make delicate lines on parchment or canvas with a pen or a brush. No brother, for me it is too late'.

One day, to pay homage to Albert for all that he had sacrificed, Albrecht Dürer painstakingly drew his brother's abused hands with palms together and thin fingers stretched skyward. He called his powerful drawing simply 'Hands', but the entire world almost immediately opened their hearts to his great masterpiece and renamed his tribute of love 'The Praying Hands'.

Dürer's masterpiece mirrors the story of sacrifice, generosity and selflessness, told in the lives of parents, teachers, good neighbours and many friends. Our resilience, courage and generosity are a reminder that we can truly embrace the possible. The most vulnerable and wounded parts in our lives, like Albert's wounded hands, can indeed be our most sacred beauty.

20

Let go to begin again: an invitation for us all

As we journey through life we often unknowingly find ourselves letting go of things, of emotions, of friendships and indeed loved ones. In many ways life itself is a continuous process of letting go in order to begin again. This process begins with birth itself – letting go of the warmth and safety of the womb in order to embrace and begin the experience of life in the world. Letting go is a part of every step on the journey of our human condition and brings with it all the emotional experience that accompanies us on our fragile pathway.

At times letting go can be easy or even something to look forward to. We move on from our studies to a workplace that has new opportunities. However, more significant moments of letting go are much more challenging and can be a painful process and hugely emotional process.

Letting go doesn't mean we don't care. Letting go

doesn't mean we shut down. Letting go means we stop trying to force outcomes or to make people behave in the way we would like them too. It means that we stop resisting the way things are. It means that we stop trying to do the impossible, trying to control that which we cannot, and instead focus on what is possible, taking care of ourselves. We do this with as much gentleness, kindness and love as possible.

Often we find that it may be very difficult to let go. We hold fast by letting go. We become something new by ceasing to be something old. For me, this is close to the mystery that is life itself. I once visited a very wise elderly person who had reflected a lot on the mystery of life and I wrote down a very powerful statement that she expressed close to her death.

'I know no more now than I ever did about the far side of death as the last letting go of all, but now I know that I do not need to be afraid of not knowing. God knows that all matters'.

The greatest thing at any moment is to be willing to give up who we are in order to become all that we can be. This is a very hopeful invitation that is realised through God in our lives. We all need to let go. Many of our lives may be bruised or indeed weighed down by baggage that limits our desire and potential for freedom and contentment. In this regard, there is an enormous desire for healing in all our hearts. Healing is that very beautiful process of letting go in order to begin again in the new life and opportunities that God gives us this day.

The Serenity prayer is a gift for us all.

God grant us the serenity to accept the things we cannot change, the courage to change the things we can and the wisdom to know the difference.

21

Our Lady of Perpetual Help

The following prayer is a very powerful one, a prayer I grew up with in Carlow Cathedral during the annual solemn novenas to Our Lady of Perpetual Help. These novenas were a time of great blessing and grace when God's spirit anointed the prayers of his people with those wonderful Christian virtues of faith, hope and love.

O Jesus, we believe in you, we hope in you, and we love you.
Strengthen our faith, renew our hope and love, and grant our prayers.
Touch with your healing love, O Lord, all who feel the hurt of life's wounds.
Long ago, when people prayed to you for healing,
You listened to them, blessed them,
And answered their prayer.
Heal us now of our sinfulness
And of the hatred that divides us.

Take away our hardness of heart.
Open our eyes, which are often blind to the needs of others.
Remove our selfishness and our greed.
Give us self-control at all times, and fill our hearts with your eternal love.
O Jesus, we ask you now to heal and bless us, and fill us with your peace.
Amen

Over the years I have helped to coordinate a novena to Our Lady of Perpetual Help in various parishes. The iconic image of this devotion is a powerful one: a young child in his mother's arms, comforted and assured despite the horrific images of his future passion and death, which angels around him are holding.

In my life, devotion to Mary has been a source of comfort and blessing. She is a gentle intercessor, always available, whispering my needs into the ears of her beloved son. I pray the rosary daily. It helps me to enter into the mystery of God's presence.

I'm attracted to Mary because of her great courage and generosity. Mary's yes was given wholeheartedly when she responded to an angel's invitation to be the mother of God's Son. In the same spirit, Mary listened to Gabriel's inspirational and positive words, 'Nothing is impossible to God'.

Part of the annual novena to Our Lady of Perpetual help is gathering thousands of petitions from those who attend. In 2016, our nine-day annual novena was attended by thousands of people in Portlaoise. The petitions they presented were very much the 'meat' of our prayer. They were heartfelt petitions, often from mothers praying for blessing and healing upon their families. I try to ground this devotional formula with a guest speaker giving a testimony about he or she finds God's presence in the bits and pieces of daily life. Personal testimony is key to evangelisation, ordinary people witnessing extraordinary faith and healing.

Mary is a woman who challenges us. She looked beyond her own comfort at a young age when she went to help her cousin Elizabeth in her need. In the same ways she challenges me to never look inward or become blinded by the comfortable. The image of Mary at the foot of the cross is both heartbreaking and comforting. Her heart must have bled to see her son in agony, but her joy was great when he rose from the dead, victorious over the powers of darkness and oppression. Mary ponders things in her heart and we can all emulate her contemplation.

Sometimes in life we don't have the answers or even the right words. The beauty of cultivating a personal relationship with God is that no verbose formulas are necessary in order to converse with him. My greatest spiritual conversations happen in the silence of my own heart.

Mary is blessed with trust. 'Do whatever he tells you'.

Trust is indeed a spiritual gift; it is an innate understanding that no matter what, all will be well. I'm sure that deep down Mary was greatly alarmed during that family wedding she attended with her son Jesus. In Cana, her son was about to perform a miracle but such a sign would bring him closer to confrontation with authority. To say that she must have had mixed feelings is an understatement. But her spiritual trust transcended her human fear, leading to the necessary transformation and spiritual blessing that turned water into wine. The transformation we need may be fear transformed into hope, sickness into health, debt and unemployment into new opportunity.

Mary is both a role model and source of protection in my priesthood.

22

Prayer of gratitude to God

Father, dear Father,
I am so grateful for everything that you have given me.
Thank you so much for the loved ones in my life,
For the many ways in which I am cared for and supported.
Thank you for the many ways I can serve and give to others.
Thank you for the rich tapestry of colours in creation,
For the beauty which is all around me,
For the skies and the ever-changing cloud formations,
For the breath-taking sunsets and early morning mists.
My heart is so grateful and brimming with thanks.
I could write a thousand books about your great goodness,
And still have many stories to tell.
I thank you from the bottom of my heart.
I thank you with everything I am.
All my being cries thank you, Lord!
Amen

Leabharlanna Poibli Chathair Baile Átha Cliath
Dublin City Public Libraries